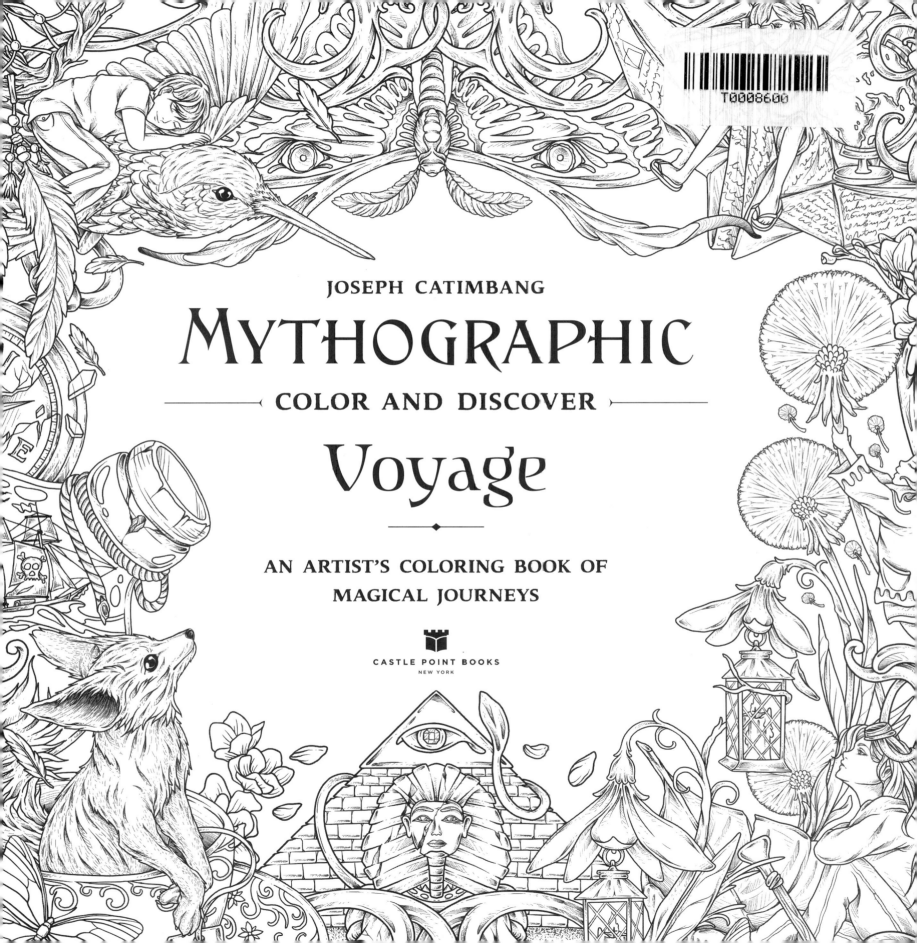

JOSEPH CATIMBANG

MYTHOGRAPHIC

COLOR AND DISCOVER

Voyage

AN ARTIST'S COLORING BOOK OF
MAGICAL JOURNEYS

CASTLE POINT BOOKS
NEW YORK

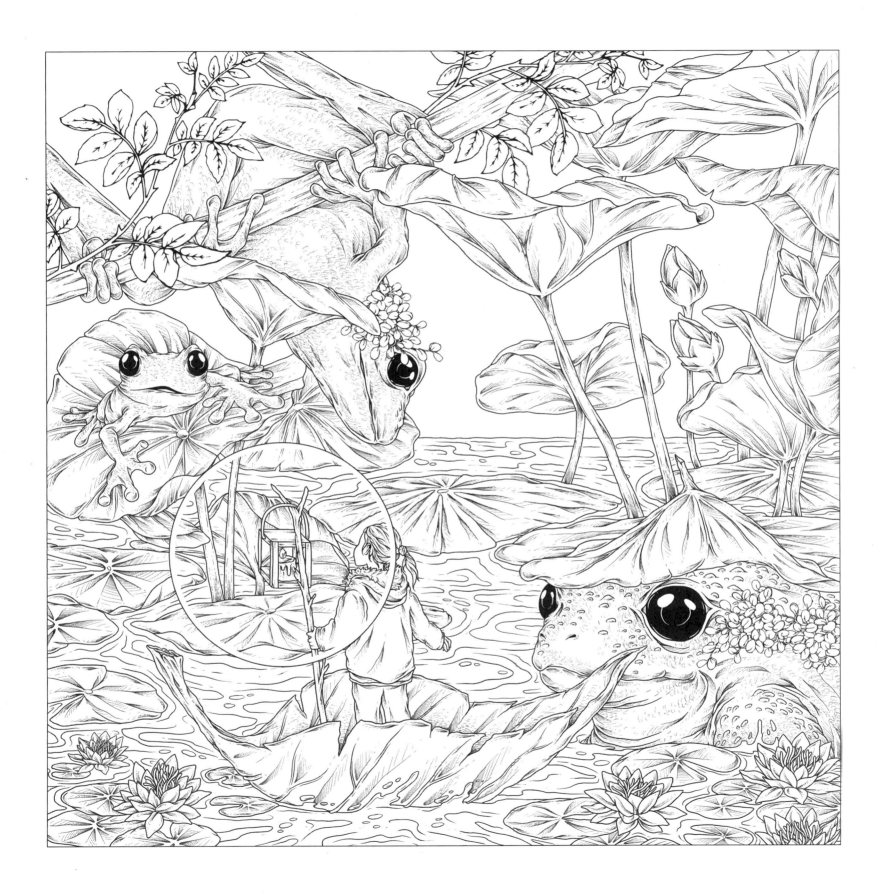

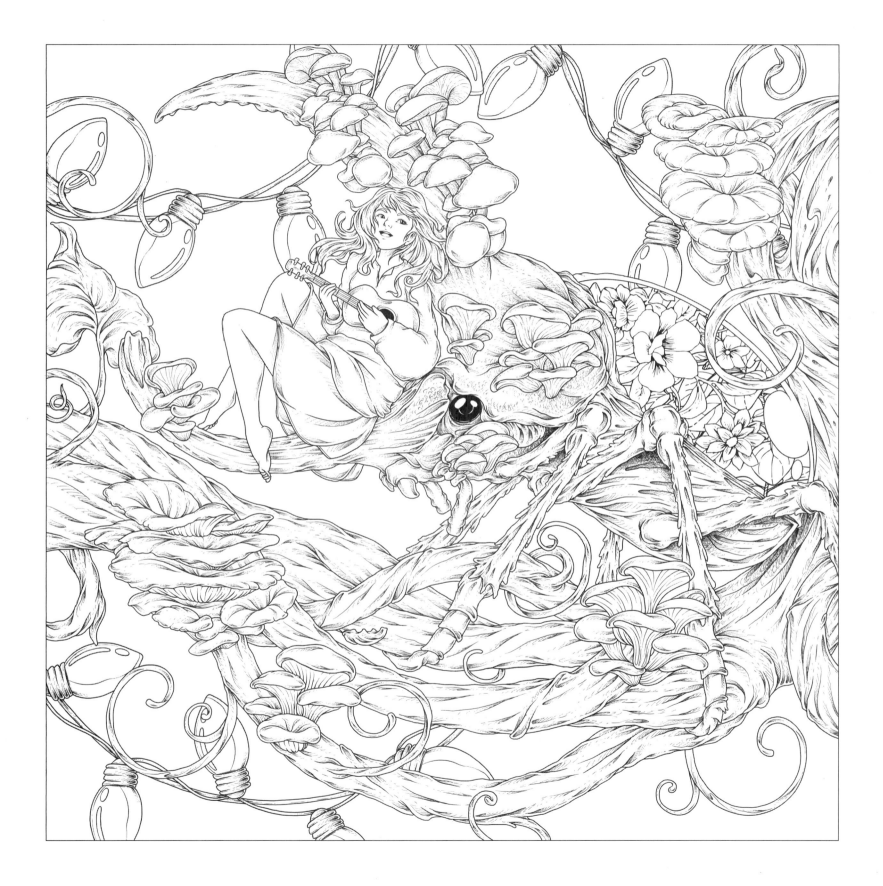

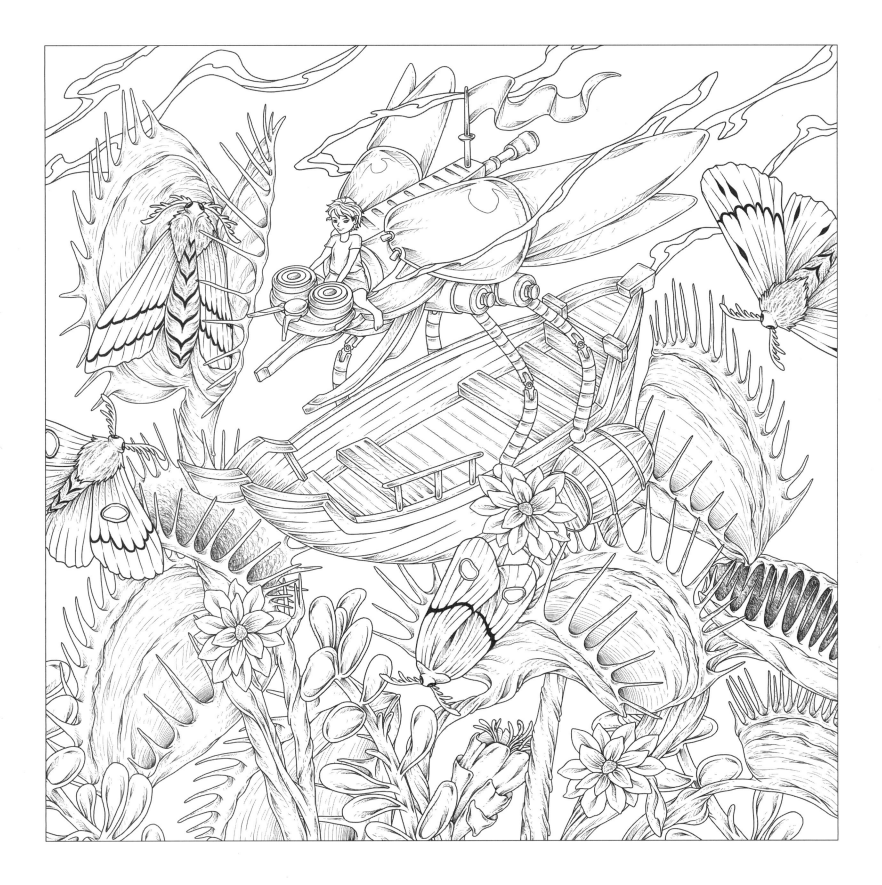

Discover more of Mythographic

MYTHOGRAPHIC COLOR AND DISCOVER: VOYAGE.
Copyright © 2022 by St. Martin's Press.
All rights reserved. Printed in Canada. For information, address
St. Martin's Publishing Group, 120 Broadway, New York, NY 10271.

www.castlepointbooks.com

The Castle Point Books trademark is owned by Castle Point Publishing, LLC.
Castle Point books are published and distributed by St. Martin's Publishing Group.

ISBN 978-1-250-28179-1 (trade paperback)

Cover design by Young Lim

Our books may be purchased in bulk for promotional, educational, or business use.
Please contact your local bookseller or the Macmillan Corporate
and Premium Sales Department at 1-800-221-7945, extension 5442,
or by email at MacmillanSpecialMarkets@macmillan.com.

First Edition: 2022

10 9 8 7 6 5 4 3 2 1